Kin tsu gi

Kin
tsu
gi

Isi Unikowski

PUNCHER & WATTMANN

First published in 2022
Published by Puncher and Wattmann
PO Box 279
Waratah NSW 2298

https://www.puncherandwattmann.com
web@puncherandwattmann.com

ISBN   9781922571458

Cover design by David Musgrave
Typesetting by Morgan Arnett
Printed by Lightning Source International

A catalogue record for this work is available from the National Library of Australia

This project has been assisted by the Australian Government through the Australia Council, its arts funding and advisory body.

Australian Government

Australia Council for the Arts

For Rachel and Jack
Alexander and Miriana
And especially for Lidia

Contents

a pebble for the quiet place

the stillness of things happening elsewhere

A Jokoban
(Japanese incense clock)

A smouldering grid on a cypress stand
jasmine interval, periods of patchouli
musk and camphor schedules, frankincense chimes.
How arid the reliance
on an oscillating crystal's precision
the tiny force between wheel train
and escapement, a miniature replica
of how the engines of our minds
or lives have been shunted together,
industrial clank for a heartbeat.

Instead, imagine saying *I'll meet you*
when it turns sandalwood, I'll get to it at myrrh;
had we but cedarwood enough, etc.

A different self stands outlined
in the doorway of the senses
that remembers childhood as a music box
its formal stations replaced by the dairy horse
before dawn, newspaper boys' cries, postman's whistle
ice-cream vans playing *Greensleeves*
siren at shift's end from the factory over the creek
a crystal radio's static.

Once, trudging home from your first job
you turned into a row of shops somewhere
you'd never been before, and looked up
at their dingy, Victorian façade, followed
their pilasters and cornices to the top floor,

its dusty mullions half lost
in low, hanging mist that ever since
feeling it on your face
has evoked the future's possibilities

saying *it will happen in light drizzle.*
We could use *luminous*
to mean all the possibilities of time read backwards
like eyes in old photographs
reflecting the future's oncoming headlights,
as I squint to read the watch on someone's wrist
standing amongst the camel's-hair coated lot
smiling from the mantelpiece; or lit up as the distant town hall clock
my brother and I competed to see from our vinyl crow's nest,
the friendly utility of its hypotenuse.

Time released by burning grains
doesn't unwind but is brought to us
as if by kings in bivouacs across the desert's electric zones.
From the creak and crease of their saddlebags
they place sandalwood and myrrh beneath
hoists glimmering in back yards
reflecting the Southern Cross directly above.

'Of the fruit of the tree...'

Did it (as she reported in that flap of a note
hanging on the fridge) taste good to her?
What mystery was she trying to convey,
what was she looking for
in the gold mantle between skin and stone?

　To eat an apple, leaving others behind
　since one could hardly eat them all, seems
　unremarkable, a gesture, hardly a sin.

To eat every plum was a fruition,
a challenge to the notion they were his to be taken.
She said nothing. He was none the wiser
judging by the lack of any answer.

　He knows nothing of the way it whispers to her —
　blackwash in the foliage
　floating nightbuoy
　where the branches are thickest
　where all the stories converge
　where the darkness at its centre speaks.

　　In our growing knowledge of where we were heading
　　we planted a tree that would always be early
　　into budbreak, early into leaf-fall
　　becoming a different shape while last year's lingered
　　fretwork in the frost.

Anyway, he had no idea what was in the fridge,
never regretted what could be replaced through those snaplatch years.
But she was dismayed by how much could be taken

Somehow the way she holds the dimpled sphere
the tender token of its corona
seems to fit the fable better than the apple's bitter seeds,
its spat success, strewn before strife, before war.

Sparks sprang from my mattock like a gangster's matches.
Still, it grew: backweird limbs determined to cross
even as they carved into one another. Yet you mourned
every pruning: how could I not love a tree so dear to you?

so she leaves this note on the fridge, saying
she's sorry she's eaten all the plums et cetera…
thinking of another life they might have led,
she says sometimes,
testing him, testing them:

They don't peer back, shoulder to shoulder, into the gold haze.
No celestial font, no blazing escutcheon
sees them off, their departure unproclaimed,
yet still the past seems to speak to them,
unbidden, from another room
in a silent house:

Heartstock. Dark fruit amongst the darker leaves.
Summer ends with a thunderstorm, a gold and purple flourish
you angrily sorting detritus in the shed
me watching from the kitchen
the sparse and speckled savour
of antique words in my mouth:

forgive me

I have eaten

At the Broinowski Gate

A busload of adolescents and bureaucrats trade frisbees
dispelling the parterre's formality. The design emerges
only when they leave: determined bights
for the older varieties, and then, in longer tines,
some climbers and the flash of floribunda.
A tennis court behind its arbours.

An autumnal gust curls the afternoon's corners
like an old photograph. For a moment,
it's 1951: a million minds are summoned
to great squares, throngs approach history's ramparts

but that "thin, querulous fellow" sees,
laid out in the paddocks' blank hansards,
spread before the hills' dusty asperities
a hedged, a decorous passion:
procedures laid out,
protocols bedded down
etiquette clasped in green sepals
the carmine calyx unfolding
at a subscribed nation's heart.

Harvester

The car's dorsal wave carves off
a place neither here nor there; the highway's
undertow drags at details

threshed from their commerce, tricked
into shapes elemental as furniture
in a house where we lived as children.

Cockatoos kaleidoscope
in frantic tessellations
beneath morning's cellophane moon

white on grey swerving over pallid paddocks
as if the high cloud had been shredded
by the landscape's languid gestures.

Cabins rust in dewy lineaments
their bulk emerging broad-backed
like cattle at dawn: knife guards and rasp bars

dragged from their duties, augers
forgetting their harvest, the conveyer chain
a tilde over their stilled senescence.

Only the gatherer belt insists on a fit
purposive as a flint chip
as if knowing that the sun —

like a chorister's high note,
a pinpoint on the cutter bar,
in this field under dawn beside the highway —

will always shine through.

Grammar lesson

There should be a name for the special case
in which we say '*the crowd marveled*'
if that roar that rose
over the back of the stadium walls,
over the rain-shingled streets
conveys the sense that what mattered
on the pitch, or the court, happened
in the eyes that watched it

that indicates a place has changed
for our having stood there
sheltering from the headlights' dazzle
under a descant of wet leaves
the better to watch a harvest moon

that means *this place is trying to tell you something;*
not to the undergraduates howling at Halloween
not to the dog-walkers who look up as they pass, and nod,
but to us, as we stand there to marvel
at that red corsage pinned to a foreign sky
above staircases twined
like DNA toward kitchen lights
shining through the transom windows.

The last fish and chip shop this side of town

A filament lighting a dark bulb of shops,
the long counter and behind it hot plates
and vats stretching into light out of
the rain. A row of customers waits,
hands behind backs in the line's cheerful democracy
under a calendar of three years ago, promising

lawns mowed
pharmaceuticals and cosmetics dispensed
ohms revived.

The one celebrity allowed, a grandchild's photo
peeps out from behind the till, a plastic jar of lollypops
and a buxom biker molesting a Chiko.

Meanwhile, Pete's distracted patter goes on, pencil stub scratching
on a fat pad: '*so what have youse got planned
for the weekend?*'

Regulars check in to a conversation that goes on for months:
too public for confession, too brief for consolation,
settled as a psalter.

He is the other ferryman,
the one who brings you back;
who slaps an obolus on the counter for you
as if to say
belonging is still possible.

Someone holds the door open and we step outside
to children drawing ancient shapes
in the darkness with their sparklers
and with tiny lights on their sneakers.

5 AM

Only a currawong dialing the neighbourhood
only the moon I heard ring off the glass mountains
morning thrown like a newspaper
over lawns riffled as oyster beds.

No car here starts simply, without a cigarette,
without grinding its teeth.
The world adjusts itself,
an actor readying before the lights come on.

The clatter of a runabout motor,
recognisable but detached from its source
winches upwards on its rickety scaffold of sound
balanced on the lake's soft platform.

Someone on the early shift hurries for the bus;
their slender gesture of obedience,
fingers to ears, nothing more
than the retention of an earpiece.

At Stromlo

To see what might happen a moment from now you would need
    a device so acute
it would take all meaning from time
    a machine so cold
it would bring the very laws of being to a standstill
    an apparatus so wide
it would trap a filigree of dreams drifting in from un-named galaxies
    lenses ground so finely
they would be pitted by an infant's breath a hundred miles away.

If that moment appeared, if we had just
a glimpse on a day like any other —
the kids in the neighbours' pool,
a load of rubbish taken to the tip,
the long dolly shot tracking down the weekend —

it would be as if the earth's core spilt
its yoke in hectic embers,
creeks alight with flowing stone
the grasses' copper cordage
burned to bare rock
smoke effacing pylons and fences
the great instruments a blistered melt
torn from their plinths
azimuth crumpled, cradle bereft
scorched window frames
easels for the flayed scrub
leaving only pebbles trickling
from tilting shorelines of schist
like coloured frames
in a child's encyclopaedia.

Faces turned upwards like satellite dishes,
we search for that moment,
and the next,
our patience gloved in a scree of starlight.
Our scratchy transmissions rise
like blown cinders
looping in lanyards
around the cat's-cradle constellations;
souls, like laws,
dark matter between galaxies.

A Western suburb

People who spoke from the side of languages
arrived along this haft of highway,
a bow sending semis dopplering southwards
the hollow tin of their passing
a single fact queried only by the creeks
sunset tendered in their reeds
to the saltworks' desolate ziggurat,
the city's distant barcode.

They laid bricks on clay that rose and fell
as if the swamps, newly named,
still clotted at the doors; fenced off
miniature replicas of fields back home,
places for seeds that had made their own travel plans
espaliered by lore, forever marred
by the wrong kind of rain and the wrong
kind of heat at the wrong time of year.

They bought grapes from the back of lorries
in puddled, pitted vacant lots
where factories once stood, from men small
and dark as sultanas; sampling
the dark little clouds, pushing them askance
to the tongue's tip, to the side, splitting
and spitting the skins, nodding at those ready
for miraculous vintages where each year
is worse than the last.

Wives pined for countries that no longer existed,
drawers, like quarrels with history, never quite sorted.
Still, a consolation of sorts took place too:
the kids learned the dialect (but
answered in English), its inflections
part of the apparatus of small projects
— like the lugs, flanges, block and tackle,
pop rivets, self-tapping screws — by which yards
and lives are changed, tinkering
in sheds beneath tinkling ironies of hooks,
years twisting like children held up for a neighbour.

They left their wives and daughters to a reticent grief,
a dwindling group of friends huddled on a knoll
beside the unrelenting highway,
trefoiled and plaited there like their stories
of priests and documents,
children and conscripts
crossing the unfathomable fields and forests of the past;
stories that I didn't understand, who scoffed at stories
often told, who missed the point in the telling.

The freight train's rhythm dissects the long nights.
Demijohns lie half decanted, pulleys half hoisted,
the shed door half ajar, as though someone who had gone
for a spanner was about to come out; buffets and tallboys and cots
ageing into their own honey-coloured epochs.
Only a panel, here or there, splits from time to time
in the uncured circumstances of a dry climate.

Applewine

i.m Rude Hrvatin

Dropping jokes like shelled nuts along a path
only he can discern, my wife's uncle
takes us past stands of oak and wild cherry
beyond the shy village with one surname,
greeting women who are bent over furrows
or walking home with hoes over their shoulders.

   (I'm thinking of protracted paddocks
   squared away in shire offices
   back home)

Drinking from a creek, he shows us how to fish
making traps with his fingers splayed among the dark roots.
In its bachelor's austerity his house huddles around
a voracious stove; outside
things are dried, ground, fermented, hung,
threshed from the carapace of their forms.

   (I'm thinking of the dishevelled rout
   of my splintered firewood, unsure of the grain,
   persuasion bouncing off the resinous core)

Not speaking his language and he not speaking mine,
we never exchange a word, like silent actors
losing our careers over the edge of sound

but I do have his recipe for applewine:
the removal of lees, clarification, dealing
with the must, the final racking and decanting

(I'm thinking of the self on display
in dark aquaria of conferences and offices)

the trick, he explains to my wife,
being in the patience to distil
   to distil
        to distil
             and then to distil again.

Istria

The line between white sky and white sea has faded
like the street signs of the old republic.
The bay's glittering meniscus unfurls in the breeze,
dry as the brittle leaves in your blind aunt's garden.

Bench tilted back to the sun-plastered wall
I listen, without following, to your conversation;
consonants echo in the stone house
like the juice of some dark, heavy fruit.

Along the beachfront, the drab bunting
of refugees' scarves flaps from the peeling
pastel facades of the last empire.
A taxiboat zips and unzips the harbour.

Yesterday, on a bus journey to the south,
the driver and passengers stopped for a smoke, hunched
in their leather coats, while we wandered.
We found a winged lion, etched into
the crumbling keystones of a deserted village,
laying claim to its austere hinterland,
to the alleys you translate for me. Days are more difficult:

each place and moment form the real fluency,
a different wine that slides differently around the tongue
received and lost as the line
between sky and sea – like that taxiboat
as it zips up the harbour.

Balloon season

Canberrans congregate in all seasons but especially this one.

As warm fronts sulk against flywire isobars,
crowds pause between flowerbeds in ritual commiserations of
    rainshadow,
to take in the clarity of that hessian light, or to watch galaxies
gritty with wheatbelt sand in carpark observatories.

But now thundercloud spinnakers turn the ridges' prows
into the pinewind: summer is checked.
Tussock paddocks are flecked with mist.
Balloon flotillas, flung like exclamation marks
across dawn's archipelagoes

alarm dogs with their exhalations. "Come on!" you said, taking my
    hand,
"I want to see them land!" But they seem to speed up

as they near the ground, as if coming in to land
were to gather all remaining time's drifting tethers.

Last ferry to Macau

Perhaps because somewhere in some cove
there's a deity
misplaced in its cabinet
petulant at its neglect

a breeze came up
the engines seemed louder
pushing against a swell
that seemed to rebuke the lives of all on board

one by one the passengers reached
for paper bags in the seat pockets
retching loudly, dramatically
with pitch and timbre

'I thought they were used to this'
my wife complained, but this was
a congregation united in its appalled contemplation
of malign interference, a fugue of wretchedness

until, to comfort her baby
a mother started singing, softly
in what sounded like a local dialect
the baby quietened down

an old woman in the next aisle wiped her eyes.
"I didn't think anyone sang those songs anymore" she said.
The other passengers, one by one
stopped to listen

stared out at the haze
where tiny islands were fading
back into the pallor
buoys like rings on their rocky outcrops

winking between barge lights
and somewhere, further back,
gantries and installations
where even the wind has borders

Sheep graziers alert

Frost has laid its nightly siege:
washing poised in awkward corrugations,
stiff and steaming beneath the hoist;
a fernery stencilled in salt over the windscreen,
lace fans dropped where the glass table fades
into the air's silver corridor.
The protea's bronze chevrons brushed upwards
like a raptor's feathers.

Across the southern tablelands,
farmers are doing what they need to, and can,
whatever it is that they do
when they're summoned:
move ewes and lambs, I suppose, spread feed,
hold off shearing…I don't know, although
a half hour's drive from here would take me
into a formal setting of white damask, fences
sage as the blade on a moon-dial's marble.

Heater on full, I would stare at the distant caped figures,
intent on bales beside bright, green tractors
that are all the greener for the pale slopes on which they stand,
cattle sprayed like ink across the parchment paddocks.
And think of people, elsewhere: scattered,
dying of thirst and shame
on distant, freezing hillsides.

Holbrook

As if to emphasise the artifice of location
the town's outskirts barely serve as that:
the stillness of things happening elsewhere.

Bales of shade stacked under the long verandahs.
Children from the station-wagons ticking by the kiosk
cling like aphids to a submarine that rears
above the carpark, heading out to where
cows are consulting the stringybarks.

　　　　　Three o'clock.
Heat rises like fumes from bowsers, the brick
bulk of the Boys' Club. A straw baker
slumps against yesterday's blackboard specials.
Between the antiques emporium and the stock agent,
the hotel, propped high on its forepaws,
watches the fences behind the mechanics' institute
scraping paddocks into stubbled schemes.
Willows lean in veteran etiquette towards
an advertisement for tea that occupies the whole side of a house,
confident as its era of brown satchels labourers used to carry for their
　　lunch,
bands on shunters' fedoras.

If we no longer see miracles performed, it may be
because we no longer haggle with divinities.
My grandfather, believing the sun had to shine
on its birthday, at least once, always saw it shine
on a Thursday, and here it is! A monstrance for the route
sharp and high as the lovely, keen places

of the mind, as if the sky were a mirror, shattering
in the sparks from a welder's torch that flare
from a dark doorway.
    Look around, look up:
the sun ploughs the absurdities of destination
and departure, becomes a rotunda, a point
to the highway's exclamation mark.

In the rear-view mirror, the stars are wound
from west to east, a glimpse of thunderclouds
shucked like a tarpaulin from the distant ranges
as if the sky had frayed
revealing what was
and what is to be
receding darkly
beneath.

Eremitani, Padua

What a civilization puts up on a wall and what it tears down
are assembled here as priorities on both sides of the equation:
a barracks, a main-line station, munitions dump;
an apse, a rose window, emotions countenanced for the first time.
First at the site to tot up the damage
and record that we're now plus or minus a fresco or two,
the *professore* gives orders below the ruined nave
while his students hurry to crate the tares of war.
Where sagacity would suggest desertion or neglect,
his successors minister to our talents:
people still smashing antiquity's nose, setting landmines
on the roads that cross the checkpoints from past to present.
Outside, as we leave, dropping coins into the honesty box,
five Africans are sleeping in the courtyard,
spooned against their neighbours' backs for warmth,
the baubles of their livelihood abandoned on the threadbare blankets.

Logo

When at last the bucktooth grin of its grille emerges from the traffic
and my mother and I board the bus to take us into town
I'm busy explaining to her how ailerons work but
looking at the crimson piping on the driver's dark blue uniform
passengers smiling at my expertise
and at the signs inserted in wooden frames down the aisle
the logo of *The Melbourne and Metropolitan Tramways Board*
a promiscuous entanglement of capital letters' arms and legs
bulbous ends and elbow crooks
that proud, first definite article
arms outstretched, propped up, a canopy
over a disassembled skeleton of letters
laid across and behind one another
so that as the eye moves across them
one letter, then another, moves into prominence or retreats
each in slight relief and gravitas
from a thin shadow that curves with the inner spaces
and what looks like a preserve jar clip round the outside
to hold it all together, giving
elegance to the design
and to the journey of those
who never had to travel far.

Even joy has its coordinates

Not that hard to remember, or even to place
where it happened. But to begin
with a human thing: all that I can see of it now
is light held along surfaces, shaped by edges.

Where and when it happened begins
with a meeting I had arrived early for,
watching light held along surfaces, shaped by edges,
gold flakes settling in sunshine's green glass, a morning

I had arrived early for. The meeting
wouldn't start for an hour or so, so I sat outside
in the morning, sunshine like gold flakes settling in green glass,
reading something I'd meant to get to in a moment like that.

For an hour or so I sat outside,
alone among leaf-bedecked tables, stacked garden chairs
reading something I'd meant to get to in a moment like that.
What seems important now, what places me there

alone at a leaf-bedecked table, un-stacked garden chair
is not some stuff I half remember in highlighter, scribbled margins,
what makes that of so many places I have been seem important
is a wave, slower than thought, cloudier than feeling.

Lurid highlights and scribbled margins
can't recall it, because there's nothing to be done with it
that wave, slower than thought, cloudier than feeling:
something passing overhead had settled momentarily.

When I can recall it, I don't know what to do with that
knowledge that it passed as I moved through it.
Something passing overhead had settled momentarily
and I just happened to be there for it.

It had passed even as I moved through it
the way, through the gate, I could see branches moving, clouds,
    shadows.
I happened to be there for it,
and then, I guess, it had someplace to be, and me – somewhere else.

Away through the gate, I could see branches moving, shadows
of clouds captured as they fell by the things they fell upon
and now, I guess, I'm somewhere else, and it has someplace else to be,
changed by its coordinates. Joy remains

captured as it falls by those whom it falls upon,
a human thing: all that I can see of it now
is that, unchanged by its coordinates, joy remains
not that hard to remember or even to place.

kintsugi

Kintsugi ('to patch with gold') is a Japanese art form comprising
the mending of broken pottery using lacquer mixed or coated
with powdered gold... to create striking visual effects, ...[adding]
a sense of time, memory and honour to these objects

(Chittock, H. (2020). Pattern as patina: Iron Age 'kintsugi' from East
Yorkshire. In Danielsson I. & Jones A. (Eds.), *Images in the making:
Art, process, archaeology* (pp. 149-167). Manchester: Manchester
University Press.)

Exeunt

The paddocks present blind flanks to the sun
and to the two of them, the storm king
(a little winded) and his daughter. Silent, unaware
that her needlepoint art
has unstitched the moment's design,
she helps him
with his intricate, familiar coat, its pattern today
gold-finialled clouds, impasto sky.

Following the track along evening's channels
he thinks he recognises those clouds
from old movies where they billow behind villages,
over moors, silent as the soundtrack
except for the projector's pulse.

Lights come on
like diadems in lit crescents; tiny
people are moving across the rugby fields,
shouts of encouragement rising with the mist
over suburbs spilled into
late autumn's crucible.

Though assigned to its restraint the weather
reminds him he is in harness, must placate
as he is petitioned. If she bears
instruments about her ears,
he is struggling to remember the music he heard
in the body's bronze climate.

Perhaps they'll talk again when saying less
is not a weakening. For now his cry for the topsails
echoes from promontories of the past.
Her insouciant ship
tacks into a harbour of exams and friends.
For the departing audience
there is no further scene,
only loose threads of colour, threshed
and flailing
in the harried air.

A photograph of the poet as a young man

Judging by that patch of sunlight on his father's forehead
the sun must have broken through, just
as the camera captured that moment

when, perhaps, they felt that everything was going to be all right.
His father in a suit, his mother a cardigan, sash and big buttons;
arms behind their backs, smiling

as if unaware of his scowl, not fooling us by their apparent ease
the half open door behind them denying their reflection.
Time has asked the three of them to come outside for a moment.

Perhaps they have left a Scrabble game behind them
on the kitchen table, the impossible letters
from which no words can be assembled

something in his father's chest
turning over at the sight of her smile, enjoying
the game's refuge from their son's anger.

Who knows now if they glanced at one another as they went back in?
If Dad was glad to see him lying on the couch like that,
the way he used to; glad, and a little uneasy?

Or later, when he'd gone back to his digs
Mum surveyed the little yard, stared at the leaf
someone must have carried in when the photograph was taken.

Cutting lavender

From the yard's galvanised subconscious, I watch
the kids retreat, wielding cartoon Excaliburs
summoned in, like their mates, from evening that pushes
with moths' shoulders at the broken bobbins.

The sparse stalks seem to bend under its weight
but there's no regret in this small theft of a moment,
understanding more clearly how we hold
to what is least permanent.

A patina of porchlight settles on a child's silhouette,
flywire-framed, Byzantine. Perhaps these acrid tufts
emerging to the rain are like laws waiting
to unfurl in some untended allotment of the universe.

How dark the Western sky is tonight.
A massive wingbeat overwhelms streetlights.
I can only tell the wind has come up
because the lavender is trembling, its tiny movement

a beat in time with the Pleiades scudding
like sleep across the lawn
ever clearer for being seen
from the corner of my eye.

'You never said it's a race, Dad!'

Oh, but it's a race all right, trust me, kid, that
hill he almost managed to beat you to the
top of ("Rubbish!") challenged him more than you, de-
spite all the picnic

stuff he made you carry in your Batman rucksack.
It's a race to find all the spare parts, becoming
antiques, puzzling kids in the bike shop while you've
multiplied years like

gear ratios; slipping cables, missing
chain links, pedals going around faster but the
landscape's keeping pace with his hunched shadow
even though you're nudging his

rear wheel; love ballasts his panniers.
You imagine the peloton behind you, scattered by your
wake; while his has vanished round the next un-
fathomable bend.

The jugglers

In the warm dusk, pink and purple arcs
appear above the old town's lanes
as jugglers toss their clubs outside
a gallery's bright, acrylic interior.
Petunias lean from baskets like cheerful spectators,
carriage horses wait in plumed rows
for tourists from the ship that dominates the wharf
below. A couple and their son pause
with the laughing crowd.
He allows himself to be photographed
against a fresco, along with trappers, traders and explorers.
    — *How thin he seems beside those ramparts…*

His parents, under strict instructions not to look back
to see if he is following
look back
but he has turned away
he has become hard to find in the shadows
at the audience's edge.

Lights flicker and shift on his face
as he stares at a juggler's jeweled midriff.
But he too is conjuring
glass constellations that glitter in his mind
an arc of possibilities thrown across the warm night sky.

What are they worth, those dreams
if they don't burn like acid,
if they are not as heavy as uranium,
if they don't scatter like quicksilver, only to return
when the rain, like a child,
brings its neighbourhood to your door?

'To be quiet and not crush'

To be quiet and not crush
the little paper aeroplanes of your sleep
I have witnessed and rehearsed the slender defection of your
    belongings,
as if the moon's paparazzi flash
through the blinds made a negative of our lives.

The white square
that will fall if the door handle turns
is not a blouse;

that long, smooth box
left too close to the edge
not your glasses case;

rockpools over which I stumble
toward morning's long shore
not your shoes.

A tray opens its unkempt hand,
no longer able to hold the sift
of diffident, indifferent years.

No matter how slowly I move,
make my Balinese dance between furniture, I betray
their fidelity, their regret for us, our hard edges.
At my touch their banked life wakens
from starlight's gilt album.

Photo of a girl with her cat

Suddenly, there it is, creased by its travels,
reappearing after all this time, a photo
of a girl cradling her kitten
moments before, startled by the flash,
it clawed and would have jumped. Except —
with a little cry of pain or dismay
that something so yearned for should so quickly
have become a reality to be managed as it fought to escape
— you carried it safely back indoors.
                       Tonight, years later, grocery-
           pendulous,
I stop outside your door to listen. The night's giant screws turn
on the shaft of a laptop's sullen
murmur. Here
in the cold winds of my watch I wonder
if some part of you has found somewhere
to hide and wait it out
with that tenacity.
May all that clasps you be kind,
hold you fast to hope,
that clawed and squirming creature.

Looking for Rabbi Alexander's grave

Cloudshadow snags tussocks and scree
down the listing hillside.
Roped into helping Dad
look for the grave of a rabbi
who taught him in his childhood
anxious to please
we slither across the unthreaded slope
with no reason to look anywhere
in particular: tiny pebble tumuli
show the search for some was easier.

Perhaps there was some sort of map,
kilter or ken
for those who lived in the town below,
but in our care to avoid barely distinguishable plots
we blunder over still more ancient graves.

The grass serrations keen,
the wind holding a single note
against the hillside's arc.

The wind holds the note low and taut
like a movement of musicians' hands
that makes you aware how long that note has been held
for how many years that note held you
turning your face
to a past it had become hard to interrogate,
a note catching on sudden vistas
between tilting rows
fraying against time
that tells us of itself in stone.

On being the middle generation

After the clamour of choosing a captain
the Cobbers – barely taller than the plastic yellow stumps –
fan out in cartwheels or stare at clouds
like distant white shorts fielding the soggy sky

while the Warriors loll or abscond with their mates
to the dank, graffiti'd toilets.
Cockatoos apostrophise the oval's timber boundaries,
heavy-hoofed Dads look up ("Oh, *shot! Run*, Alex!")

from their murmured discussion of merits and means.
I'm thinking of my father's childhood, of how we need
a taxonomy, a way of mapping worlds

as if they were cousins, consanguineous,
by human alchemy intertwined
proliferating branches of acceptance and release
from exile and diaspora's inheritance.

First world: my father reading Jules Verne for his friends
in the icy ghetto; *second world, once removed*
from our kids:
unable, for fear of the racket,
to put down a zinc bucket he has carried to the attic
while the Gestapo questions people in the apartment below,
my grandfather watches a stray dog in the street outside.

That might be a way of mapping how I have come to this field,
its big face beaming upward into the Saturday drizzle
making its pitch to the sky, like a kid,
momentarily pleased with himself
for having scored a few runs.

For my daughter who complained that the sparrows woke her up

He got it wrong, that bloke who placed
these tiny sentries on the border
to proclaim no entry to the old.
We inhabit the same country,
borders defined by affection on our side,
tolerance on theirs,
as we perform for one another
through windows decanting
morning's hesitant light.

Holed up in rooms carpeted
by their misery, like soft layers
at the floor of caves,
it is the young who can only hear that song
as noise: incessant, insistent.

But gradually you will learn to listen until,
one day, these fanfare flautists will call
only to you
from thorns where they've hidden
below shadows that hover against the sun.
Tweezer-beaked, they will call you
to the grace of a single day,
unchanged, predictable.
And then, in a collage of sky-bathing windows
you will suddenly be aware of their high-jinked
angle-flit westering,
you will see
the world changing
one twig at a time.

A red rhododendron

i.m. Ivan Hrvatin

She has signed the forms in her diffident hand,
sent his suits to the Salvos;
someone in this gap time, from a distance,
has given her a rhododendron.
Still in florist's paper it stands
in the darkening hallway, a ferris wheel
of tiny red gondolas on the rim of colour,
salvage from the porcelain cold of mourning's reaches.

Fill your eyes, it seems to say,
fill your eyes with colour –
a tinnitus of air, sunset's last glimmer,
a prospect that the dead keep us in their memory
as once it was our departures that they felt more keenly:
kids pushed into the car, the thermos, that cursory wave,
our terse focus on rehearsed distances
reports along the way from neat, deserted towns.

Perhaps it's in this colour, this warmest of colours,
that we appear to them: as if, in leaving,
they had jettisoned all other hues
but this one, almost too intense to be seen,
as they look out and forwards at us from albums
in frame after frame, asking:
who have you made joyous for your standing on this earth?

I allowed myself to answer that there was a choice
between one kindness and another
or one heartache and another.

I allowed myself to ask: what does it matter?
But if it doesn't matter, who are we
that this descant of the spectrum
should so dispel our capabilities?

It should be possible to prise open the covers of his life
look in the index under 'r' for *red*
see grapes he crushed every year,
the stained press, barrels and demijohns,
the car he drove for 600 kilometres without refueling just to see if he
      could
the piano accordion he'd take out when he was happy
bits of tunes he played, really, for himself.
In the distance he has already travelled
— face less clear,
voice less heard,
hands less held —
it's still just possible to make out that gesture,
the same slight duck of the head:
listening for fermentation, a fan belt, a chord,
and his nod of approval.

And should that colour fill our eyes —
a car that, for a moment, seems about to turn into the driveway,
a dusty bottle half-buried under the house —
as that colour fills our eyes
we know we are remembered.

For Alexander, turning 13

(Numbers xiii-xv)

Your grandfather steps lightly over the cold kitchen floor
almost jauntily. Don't be fooled: he's feeling his way with his feet,
the world unfolding its bleached parchment,
hues shoaling in the lavish glare. Meanwhile, secreted
to practise your reading (dutiful, impervious, bored)
may something of its intent

remain with you: an understanding that a map of the world's contours
begins with an ascent, requires you to crest
the hill country of the heart, whence
the vast concatenation manifests.

Below you, the future's unsuspecting pastures and fences,
its cantillation of distant beacons and fire towers
spreads before you. One day, you too will have to report back, from
    notes
you might leave to yourself as a record of what you saw. Or might not.

Lullaby

Our sun-cankered, frost-lacerated old bomb
has usurped a spot beside a Milky Way of faces.
Fingers tapping on the dash, I watch
pigeons filibuster on ledges outside floors
lit by cleaners; stare at the back of my hand
charting middle age's sargassos; and finally you,
calling some last instructions
like streamers at a ship's departure,
cross to lean reluctantly by the door.
All the adages I should have draped over your slender neck
— but didn't, for fear they would hang so heavily —
are reduced to this: "How will you find me
in the dark if all your friends have left the party?"
Your laughter: "Dad, I'd recognise those headlights anywhere!"

Watchman in the orchard

A roof away
over spare tiles stacked like heaven's stumps
the big old gum's galleries are restless
with an easterly off the escarpment,
a newborn galaxy of green fireworks.
Woodchimes clack a reverie against the breeze,
click of parrots sourcing plums.
Beak down, intent, a scrivener's index finger,
a currawong probes autumn light like laid sheaves.
Its stolid derrick kowtows
to tiny packets of emolument under twigs and leaves
strewn like discarded toys around the trunk.

Watching from the porch, I wonder
what it would be like
to have that knowledge, that indifference,
sassy as its yellow eye
creasing whole suburbs down along their streets,
the faultline's bulwark seams
folding inwards into certainty,
centred as a grub.

No dream emerging from its soft case
is ever forgotten. Midnight waters
of such sweetness
that to drink them in the neon light's thin frost
is to secrete them forever.
                        So why
does the past eddy like a river
between storehouses gapped like crosswords

a crystal flash in a rose window
a movie projected too slowly,
unjoined between frames?
As if that lad, having stepped so lightly
into the story, was sent to retrieve the arrows
but dawdled, couldn't make out what they were calling,
and unable to find them,
failed to return.

                    And then
my eyes decipher what my heart has already noticed:

you have entered the room behind me
your shoulder a contour of tiny explosions of sunlight
its rays a flying buttress of completion.

There, that moment —
that must be the gauge, a spirit level
marked off by what is opened or closed,
what is crimped, clenched, circles in close,
or unfurled, bears outwards
along longitudes hung from the morning moon's sextant
new coastlines of experience
like bits of string dropped onto ancient maps

I will navigate them

nomad of the soft cities
digging at time's dwindling reefs
appealing the drilled stars
unheard as the fruit that falls
in this endless orchard.

a pebble for the quiet place

Before the manuscripts are chained

The abbot's insistent: so much to do before
snow covers the quarries and the passes are closed.
He has us at our desks before dawn; commissions
come down from the abbey every other day.
Yesterday we lost a hymnal
because the gold leaf ran too quickly: the master raged.
Artists and scribes huddle in tense corners
squabbling over designs, boys run
to keep the tapers alight, haul saffron
and chalk, stack the finished gatherings.

I step into the frost outside. The moon
has scraped the sky in readiness:
a dark time. And yet, the way dawn draws
its colours from the earth
I think of you down the dreary day.
I look at the initial drop beside its line
and think of how your hair falls beside your face;
I see the space left for "*Osculetur me*"
sharpen my quills, incise the vellum.
A catchword at the bottom of the page
has me leaning forward to hear your voice.
The awl's marks lead like tiny footsteps
to our household's industry, and I would send
far for the lapis lazuli of our skies.

Can I pour enough colour into these spaces
even if smudged by my failures of reason or spirit?
Do I need to ask, as I have asked all these years,
never needing to ask: who will end my apprenticeship?
Who will say the tiers of my learning are over, grant me
licence to proceed beyond the simplest of undertakings?
Illuminate me.

Reading 'Japanese Maple' by Clive James, West Basin, early spring

How you dazzled us, old chum, with the colour of that tree!
I look up from the page: that light you said you're exiled from
that layered frieze
settles on the lake's edge. Dinghies chip at the glaze upon
its surface from which, like cedillas, swans hang and are gone.

Nothing gains by contrast in such abundance, all's elect.
Your tree's privilege was vouchsafed by a paltry climate
where its effect
had to be constructed; its tiny trunk, every floret
(in a pot? in the ground? – you never said) had to divot

off days of whetstone grey, giving shape to separation
— from the breeze in she-oaks here, and there from time still
    wanted —
a serration,
a gentle clarity, this if nothing else: that, wintered
out, tired as you were, you still saw the tree as form, vaunted

in masculine, full rhyme, metered syllabics, the real ken.
Poetry makes even less happen these days than before,
nought to reckon
by; still — a world worth staying alive for, an embrace formed
by ten tiny leaves (except in the third line, only four).

Days of the accord

Because it was wet and neither of us felt like working,
we traced concessions on the greasy table and negotiated borders.
I was ready to relinquish epochs. You, to my fury,
quibbled over neighbourhoods. I'm sorry:

streets you bargained over were, for me, terraces
scored with washing, child-flitting alleys
that led to the old port and the sea, an imperial coin
embossed by clouds, vaults and cardos

towers rising above orchards and ravines
into sunshine, prayer
dispensed from their crenellations.
So we fall back onto studied courtesies.

Hectored and lectured between
fallen columns, how could you understand
the double failure of our auguries —
how they were used, and what we thought they portended?

Now that I have conjured you beside me in the lamplight
take off that toga, those spats, these antique graces:
all our mosaics proclaim we advance
by accommodation, for all that ancient bluster.

Grey, green, silver (elemental machinery)

I had forgotten
        rain's mechanism: how it doesn't fall
but is requisitioned, plucked from a city's plumage
that in the arrogance of its towers has forgotten to ask.
Windows peer down onto cafes
where consultants perch, their cases arranged
between tables like fat, black tails.

I had forgotten
        that only when those who are changed,
damaged, awry, stand beneath
the crabbed and burled witness of the peppermint gums,
touch the grudging tapers of their foliage,
somnolent chandeliers
lit by evening unrolling like some fabric flung
across market trestles for those who have arisen and gone
from their burnished councils;

only when hope's tiny paper boats
have navigated beyond permission's precincts

only then
does the rain begin
sheets of pewter coinage poured
into that unexpecting, unresisting lap.

Still life

It's as if all the world's ravelled, bright particulars
have streamed through a pinhole in the side
of a box, down a corridor of Delft tiles
on which tiny figures from childhood hide
from my self-portrait, ghostly in its dun
vestments, and the servant drying linen in the dunes,
making the images blurry, inverted. Details
such as these meant something to people once, they
would have recognised the tulips, citrus, overturned bouquet,
the chalice that struts on damask drapes.
Hands behind my back and from my time I gape
at the mantel, a strand of dropped
cargo, tiny figures bent to their commerce at the tendered quay.
Ships ready their serene freight;
I ponder the hourglass, insects, the gap
that puts beyond reach the risqué
hare proferred to an abandoned lute,
pewter languor of a herring on its plate,
crimson fruit chased in lattice light.

A patch of grass

(In July 2008 an earlier painting was discovered under Van Gogh's
'A Patch of Grass')

Well, why leave it there? I say, let's go the whole hog,
false starts and pentimento! That's the stuff
for a dour age convinced of conspiracies, chuffed
at every lid lifted, every error relived: why stop with Van Gogh?

Cavaliers' arms awkwardly flaunted,
a repainted stance reveals the groom's fear,
the girl with the earring's secretive leer,
feasts, dejeuners and Last Suppers haunted

by ghostly visages, doubts and scribbles.
A synchrotron: there's a fine Kolinsky sable
for the twenty-first century! Prised from their archives, every codex

is ransacked for rough drafts of the Bible,
the Pieta's armpit searched for labels,
Shakespeare scoured for the remnants of Tippex.

Jedem das seine

The slogan on the gates of Buchenwald: "To each his own"

How well I know that photograph from childhood's mantelpiece:
that line, innocent in its intent, shuffling past
a guy in a beret. A boy squints upwards into the sun
and the young man who will become my Dad

half turns away to a friend behind
forever challenging our certainty it's him.
Hard to imagine that our parents passed through such gates:
yet they are here, in a wholeness, and there

in his camp's stripes, as if still
in the shadows of the last few days' concealment.
The motionless instants behind the gate have only just begun
to meld into the sequence our present demands

that queue an arrow moving forward in tiny
fractions of time divisible by its possibilities.
From this vantage point — perhaps a tower? —
one can almost see back into the camp; but the gate

is a border: on that side, history's
giant factories await the consignment of peoples;
people are an abstraction, fate's barcode
a tattoo on their forearms. On this side

peoples are an abstract surmise,
the opened gate making literal
that slogan's behest; which, having faced
inward when the gate was closed, has become a lens

diffracting destiny into these young men's lives
as the line begins to move
and they begin to drift, to reach, to land.
Perhaps as he moved out past the gate

past the jeeps and the outraged liberators
he noticed the plume from an April mist
rising from a nearby forest
of beech trees after which this place was named.

Lakeside

This light is for saints, silk,
washerwomen and pomegranates
tablecloths like marzipan waterfalls,
a *plein air* in which you have set your easel,
made an inventory of the afternoon's offerings:
babies in palanquins parked
before gold and crimson precincts,
self-conscious honeymooners,
a bride as she gathers her train,
collecting hopes or clouds.

Reflections of the opposite shore
slide over the silver water
like a sheaf of photographs emerging from a tray.
Buildings of state scud like spinnakers.
A little plaque reminds those
who wander onto the soggy lawn
that a sculpture was erected, then buried there,
a standing interment,
a child's game dressed up as a concept: there but not there.

Like the traffic's noise that sidles like a bookie
through the reeds growing in clusters nearby,
the sculpture still has a presence
at least in the lawn's languid decline
even if what was momentarily feted on its green plinth,
its mocking notion, is unremembered
by picknickers in a tapestry of chamomile and pigeons
or those watching the pageantry of parasols
between pavilions open to the heat.

Returning late, light slants across bollards,
leans over the little bridge as if watching
the metal herons probe
the flagged path winding its way back
to the entrance. A camellia
gleams at my feet as if a star had slipped
from the night's icy, black lake.

Icaria

As always, time sieves a myth from the facts:
the city — a pith spilled from the karst —
has been pushed back into the yellow haze
despite the ships' urgent nuzzle at its quayside

as if to leave room for the farmer cutting terraces
from the bay's blue potential, a shepherd
checking for rain: all of parish life and industry
flowing up and to the left against the frame.

Over there, the local rag's society hack
focuses on a celebrity shaking hands
coaxing a raffle with a megaphone
watchful for someone important.

A school band, tuned awry like their uniforms,
trombone flaring over sausage-smoky booths
between which adolescents fumble, still half drawn
to the dodge-ems; for the third time, parents wander

past the jams and doilies, the obeisant lavender,
encyclopaedias and airport thrillers parked like veterans
in the sun, brochures on weed control
blown to the perimeter. A recruiter hands out air force caps.

A group of young men tests their harness,
anxious to be off; kit creaks and chafes
against the pulpy air; momentarily they feel
their silly age, ostentatiously check the gauges.

One falls from the sky; the others pass from our art
as from our sight; old men in leather jackets chat,
barely interrupted by the squadron's shadow
passing over the oval.

On first looking into junk-mail catalogues

If hanging up your small, white blouse should give me pause
to make the week's laundry an occasion
to wonder at your love's patient denial of the abstract,
I could do worse than watch the way you shop.
The *thisness* of it:
lingering in aisles, absently
trawling lines of touch along reality's hem.

Though each season brings its disappointments,
its neglect of sidelined demographics,
every expedition is a journey to
serendipity's continental shelf,
an invitation to come body-surf sight
beyond mere colour
a special wavelength
bright and hard as a toffee apple.

Summed up in a rack or remnants bin
that which we are as surface touching surface
that which we most are,
the one sense that distinguishes reality
from the roiling palette within

thrumming halls and arcades of cheerful intent
giving up what was lost, or hidden, something
we haven't fully understood, a flurry
in the corner of one's eye, something
we might once have known but can't recall

a language spread and settled
in surface's syntax
dimensions of self
stacked in coloured packages
across possibility's linoleum.

The rescue this time

Postcard white, the beach flatlined,
impassive witness to my growing grasp
of the undertow's elemental unfairness,
watching through a seagull's pale eyes
my floundering embarrassment
at having to signal for help
as I was pulled down baffling sandbanks
into the dark green ledgers.

So many mornings now feel like that:
a dark seam stains the baize calm,
carries me from sunny latitudes over
the world's edge to map's end
where the coastline falters.
Reef-surf beats at my temple:
always approaching, intent,
the scrubby, littered court a foundry yard
of bottle shards like green wavetips.
The earth swings loose in its escapement
as if I too have become an islander I read about
who woke saying 'we are heading in the wrong direction'
because of the way the current knocked against the keel of his canoe

the rescue this time
a school band setting up,
checking phones, comparing last night's swan dive
into spectacle. Flautists giggle over the arpeggio,
and then forget the hot pink socks
they chose so carefully this morning
(but Mozart doesn't)

as their gaze fixes on manuscripts
held with pegs against the breeze,
not just reading the music but allowing it to carry them
out beyond the baton, sure and unselfconscious
as that stranger's arm suddenly
lifting me, face up, seeing that seagull
still passing on its way somewhere
high overhead.

Stone suite

Terraces, Jerusalem hills

At first you hardly recognise them for what they are:
a child's flanks slowing the eye's downward trajectory,
the earth's forehead wrinkled, as if trying to remember.
Cumulus thought bubbles shadow tidepools,
slipping over forests, in and out of key.
Engineered water still runs down
cisterns and channels, then out from a stone sun
into a stream suspended
in nets of birdsong,
distracted among fallen saplings' italics
until you discern that nudge of earth,
caption in an old text face
    — the font could be Byzantine, serifs Ottoman —
to the diffident lore of borders:
something about keeping one's head down.

Chalk caves, Beit Guvrin

Standing at the base
a pillar of light
reverses the work's progress

its imperative
drawing the eyes up
to that authoritative

disk of sky until
you discern the chiselled frieze
scrolling downwards

a conversation
between sky and earth
not as deities do

in perpendicular shafts of light,
coins slashing air,
the big bang's pistons

but as things formed in twilight, revealing
themselves to be of both night
and day, emerging

between opposites,
once thought to hold something
in themselves of both

mind and the earth it touched
and therefore held to be
miraculous.

Roman remains, Bath

The pool's transcendent green, a Rothko square, seems suspended
between columns: below, in the hypocausts' portentous gloom, the
hushed congregation strains to discern the italicised labels. The
living and the plinthed, carved from or pushed for time, regard
one another. Chitons undulate, their folds insinuating the presence
within, motion in granite frames shuttered like early photography of
tightrope walkers, jugglers, someone walking in sepia sequence. These
crumbling mandibles lose their oratory while the eloquent, steadfast
eyes remain. If, by virtue of the missing head, Apollo's torso called
all the more forcefully for change, time's vandalism reminds us of his
poet: of how the lyre continued to sing in its river that has no source,

no mouth, provisioning a song that we might tell of its passage, even as we feel the grit grip at our throat, silt shoal at the entwined banks.

Mimosa Rocks, South Coast, NSW

Nobody left a sign to tell us why or when someone placed these stones on top of one another with such care: like little, rotund men staring out to sea, the way migrant Dads would stand on their patch of beach while their wives unpacked and slathered sunscreen on their kids' skinny shoulders. The stones remind me of the pebbles we leave on graves, to show we've been, but these are bigger, stacked onto one another in small cairns randomly across the beach as if a house had once leaned on them. And if, at first, I felt somehow disengaged because I couldn't tell if they *meant anything*, couldn't discern if they were as old as the midden nearby, that did get signage, or were some kind of recent claim, or artwork: well, at least someone, sometime, had found a use for this rubble (tracing the most direct line between strangers through the past: nothing's random, only a forgotten pattern) and then they'd sure been to a lot of trouble.

Werribee Park

From an ornate mirror bequeathed by the squattocracy
your father's face looks back at you. Greenhouse windows
wink on their ratchets, iron scallops held only
by a web's instance, over parterres
combed for the winter. Dutifully impressed

by the mangle's weight,
the cauldron's heaviness, the handle notched
for carrying, black blades of the stove's doors
slamming in a row like epochs, the kids sprawl
in tolerant armchairs under a deer's glassy survey;

bustles and bustiers patrol the parquetry,
deferential shadows enter from the colonnade.

Meanwhile, elsewhere: an early discharge from the Czar's army,
my great-great-grandfather's on remission
from the Crimea. Being pressganged
hasn't altered his allegiance to a higher power;
he still has to be nagged into having his picture taken
that's now all we have of him. He stands
to one side of the album, its depleting villages.

We inhabit our absences as best we can
but never, it seems, our *patch*, not as well as this:
title deeds mounted, the first sub-divisions framed and yellowing,
pointer resting on the fresco for the next school group, rooms
into which we peer from behind history's plush red velvet ropes
in all our finery: our starched fashions and fascinators
on display with the pearl-handled hairbrush,
ewers, flasks, chased caskets.

Lichen holds fast to the balustrades
its green and grey cursive repeating
like slate lessons in the schoolroom.
Time plumbs right angles from sun
to bell-tower, both mined from the same orelight
in which we make our intermittent appearance,
our arms gentle and heavy on our children's shoulders
down the gravel drive's arc towards the distant sea.

I would say something of water

of its bearing on the land
how gullies grapple with its weight
tilt into its chastened light
pearling under the sky's thumb ball
like some giant liquid metal distilled
from tors in frost-flattened paddocks
the world's blue and silver filigree.

A vertical inventory in tarn or karst,
bound in dams and bores, leashed
by levees, moved by locks and sluicegates,
water turns time into proximity;
as if what matters is the interruption
to its flow, its checked coalescence.

Once admitted, water is a fifth column
from time's icy reaches; incising
a lichen smile across granite,
it redacts the empty creek beds, rank billabongs,
granny-knot river bends so old
they have become little more than a subsidence,
the earth passing a hand over its face, as if waking up
and remembering a quarrel.

Its smallest part identical with its greatest
and therefore indivisible,
water vouchsafes no analogy,
requires no embellishment.

Water reminds me of the way
truth is figured in the world, the way truth
courses through its own gullies,
batters complacent shorelines,
rises to the gunwales of our craft.

So to the soldiers in the suburbs
to those who shared a smoke by pits
who opened files in basements
who crouched in minarets
who remembered where they had picnicked in pretty forests
and the best vantage points over the old town
who gave their names to new histories
incised on skin delicate as calligraphy on fans

I would say something of water.

Beyond the river

We crossed water before we had a name
as you did. But if our dreams trace
the rivers and seas over which we came,
it is the deserts beyond that draw us closer.

Here on Herod's porch
I can see how you were possessed
by the desert's gifts; how you learned
not to quarrel with its seasons
to draw colour, not streams, from its rubble,
from gibbers that ripened under moonlight,
to measure the riverbeds between constellations
in the splay of your hands on rock walls.

What called to us, as it called to you, had no face.
It cried "are you there?" from a sunlit bush
"are you still there?" from an acacia's solitary schwa
asked "what have you done?" of those with eyes
extinguished or aflame.

As you did, we followed water's vast pawprints
to places that became places
as they were named and lost,
stories we told our children
as they swaggered like Esau to the white verge of the tablecloth
relatives primped and propped,
worn jokes winking at the tureen.

As we did, you will cross a river
whose banks have slumped into the reeds' glib grab.
Rings of mist around streetlights
will be how your children remember camps
thumbed into the wet traffic's riverbed; malls and alleys
how they will see
the lizard's tessellated entrails
their frail translucency
words that nations around you no longer recognise as yours
mileages retirees recite from bullet-raddled road signs,
until you have all but disappeared,
giving history's joists an occasional rattle.

No columns of sunlight beckon through easy pastures beyond the river,
only a purple smudge on the horizon
that may be approaching or receding,
seems at times to be nearer, at times left behind.

Perhaps it's only a pivot of dust, salt, silt, a slick, a pan, a lull,
light lifting into serene belvederes of distance
thunder throwing its arms around the hills' bony shoulders.

Perhaps your children are dreaming
as if that acrid water still rakes their throats.

And who among the angels will find you if you move?

Unfazed by the coast road, we welcomed the challenge
of beaches heaped with wrack and kelp,
the uncertainty of estuaries gargling inland.
Neither offered nor seeking the locals' help,
we volunteered to take the King's shilling
and gusted forth in an armada of vans

to appear beside unsuspecting straits,
bearing our strange totem across blanched tundras,
down cool corridors of shade beside dry-stone lanes
or out from some eternal grimy nowhere under
a fire-escape into the midday-cambered street,
all on the assumption we had a lien

on any place with a name or GPS coordinate.
In lairy parkas or Hawaiian shirts we took our snaps;
and if sometimes the aperture missed a turning,
no-one could accuse us of a major lapse
in plying our trade: nothing made us deviate
around the patriarch and his ageing wife yearning

under the terebinth, or those doomed towns on the savannah.
Our lenses were the centre of a circle
that is everywhere; the cursor receding, as if fending
off retirees in their motorhomes, schoolkids on cycles.
We laid chevrons down on macadam like manna,
to be gathered as directions demanded; found

opportune rams in their thickets, junk food scraps,
billboards and graffiti; filled our jars
from the remorseless shaduf
of history's resentments; in chic boulevards or dusty bazaars
you could find us portrayed in antique maps
as cherubs puffing zephyrs of reproof

at the gaps left by burned, abandoned villages.
Our wings cover our eyes; your faces
grow unclear, blurred by the time we must
have spent out there, hurrying past all the places
we could not or would not go, a triage
of what had to be recorded so faithfully,
      so faithfully missed.

A pebble for the quiet place

Now with all seasons damaged under our savage dominion
it's strange to think seven people drowned here;
that water once flowed with such force
down this culvert between greenhouse cubes
of midday silence, cubbies adrift in the quiet,
slides with hands in their pockets.

Elsewhere, the past rears
on its haunches of rare marble and parquetry.
Its attendants show you reconstructed offices
with their quaint typewriters,
an ingenious system for sending documents by tube
ornately framed portraiture of our histories.

But don't be fooled: every city has its double.
You think you are familiar with these streets
that they ask nothing of you,
but until you have come here
you have only been acquainted
with one city's shared and gifted future.

At lake's end, suburbs' edge, secreted from the hubbub on the terrace,
glimpsed from the approach to the town centre,
dropped like quotation marks
the elderly use for emphasis on greeting cards,
these places have been raised from the ordinary by a silence
that stops even the marsupials from grazing here.

In a wall around the lawn, so many bricks mention *home*.
A map incised on smooth marble records where settlers' homes
became the lake that honours them.
The sandstone stele calls the children home
from the water. *Home* for those who would never find it

is painted on poles that form the outline of a boat tethered
to the safer swell of the park
where we might have known you
except for the casuarinas' deference
that sets you apart. Absences, yes, but in reminding us of loss
our home is made in the second city,

enacted through these shapes:
the smooth sides and bevelled edges of a large black block
push our gaze outwards past the lake's perimeter
as settlers watched for cloud massing over the basin.
A tall stone breaks afternoon sunlight's tilt
into a shadow that follows the watercourse.

The stonework's slope compels
the line of sight from a father who looks up
from the picnic blanket where he's sitting
to where his daughter stood a moment ago
the way people look up
when something huge is falling from the sky

.

Acknowledgements

Grateful acknowledgement is made to the editors of the following publications and websites in which a number of these poems first appeared: *Australian Poetry Anthology; Blast Furnace; Cordite; Divan; Half Way Down the Stairs; Lacuna; Lost River Review; Materiality; Meniscus; Newcastle Poetry Prize anthology; Offset; Quadrant; San Pedro River Review; 'The Disappearing' Project, Red Room; Triage; Verse Wisconsin.*

'At the Broinowski Gate' was commended for the 2009 ACT Poetry Prize; 'I Would Say Something of Water' was awarded the ACT Writers Centre Michael Thwaites Poetry Award in 2012; 'Lakeside' and 'On First Looking Into Junk Mail Catalogues' were commended for the Melbourne Poets Union Poetry Competitions in 2014 and 2015 respectively; 'Before the manuscripts are chained' was longlisted, and 'A Jokoban' was shortlisted for the University of Canberra International Poetry Prize 2014; 'Even Joy Has Its Coordinates' was highly commended for the Overland Judith Wright Poetry Prize 2017; 'Watchman in the Orchard' was highly commended for the Australian Catholic University Poetry Prize 2017; 'Of the Fruit of the Tree' was longlisted for the 2019 University of Canberra International Poetry Prize; 'And who among the angels will find you if you move?' was awarded first prize for the 2021 Yeats Poetry Prize for Australia.

Thanks to Professor Jen Webb for the publication of 'Still Life'; 'Grammar Lesson'; 'You Never Said It's a Race, Dad'; and 'The Jugglers' on the Australian Book Review's 'States of Poetry 2017' website.

I'm particularly grateful to Ross Gillett, who backed up his advocacy on my behalf with astute editorial suggestions; few poems here have not benefited from them.

Finally, of course, thanks to Dave Musgrave at Puncher & Wattmann for this publication.

www.ingramcontent.com/pod-product-compliance
Lightning Source LLC
Chambersburg PA
CBHW031002090426
42737CB00008B/642